The Life and Work of...

Claude Monet

Sean Connolly

Heinemann Library
Des Plaines, Illinois

Designed by Celia Floyd
Illustrations by Fiona Osbaldstone
Printed in Hong Kong, China

04 03 02 01 00
10 9 8 7 6 5 4 3 2 1

Library of Congress Cataloging-in-Publication Data
Connolly, Sean, 1956-
    Claude Monet / Sean Connolly.
        p. cm. – (The life and work of--) (Heinemann profiles)
    Includes bibliographical references and index.
    Summary: Introduces the life and work of Claude Monet, discussing his early years, life in London and various parts of France, and development as a painter.
    ISBN 1-57572-956-3 (lib. binding)
    1. Monet, Claude, 1840-1926 Juvenile literature. 2. Painters
—France Biography Juvenile literature. [1. Monet, Claude, 1840-1926. 2. Artists. 3. Painting, French. 4. Art appreciation.]
    I. Title. II. Series. III. Series: Heinemann profiles.
    ND553.M7C65   1999
    759.4—dc21
    [B]   99-14546
                                                                  CIP

Acknowledgments
The Publishers would like to thank the following for permission to reproduce photographs:
Page 4, Portrait photograph of Claude Monet in front of the pictures *Waterlilies* in his studio. Page 5, Claude Monet, *The Waterlilies—The Clouds*, Credit: The Bridgeman Art Library/Giraudon. Page 6, Le Havre, Credit: Bibliotheque Nationale. Page 7, Claude Monet, *The Coast of Normandy Viewed from Sainte-Adresse*, Credit: The Fine Arts Museum of San Francisco. Page 9, Claude Monet, *Caricature of a Young Dandy with a Monocle*, Credit: Giraudon. Page 11, Claude Monet, *Le Pave de Chailly*, Credit: Giraudon. Page 12, National Gallery, London, Credit: Hulton Getty. Page 13, Claude Monet, *The Thames below Westminster*, Credit: The Bridgeman Art Library/National Gallery. Page 14, Edouard Manet, *Monet in His Studio*, Credit: AKG. Page 15, Claude Monet, *Boulevard St. Denis, Argenteuil, in Winter*, Credit: Richard Saltonstall/Museum of Fine Arts, Boston. Page 16, Boulevard des Capucines, Credit: Hulton Getty. Page 17, Claude Monet, *Impression, Sunrise*, Credit: Giraudon. Page 19, Claude Monet *Entrance to the Village of Vetheuil*, Credit: Exley/Rosenthal. Page 21, Claude Monet, *Haystack at Giverny*, Credit: The Bridgeman Art Library/Hermitage. Page 23, Claude Monet, *The Cap of Antibes, Mistral*, Credit: AKG. Page 24, Rouen Cathedral, Credit: Pix. Page 25, Claude Monet, *Rouen Cathedral, Albany Tower, Early Morning*, Credit: Exley/Rosenthal. Page 26, Portrait photograph of Claude Monet and his wife Alice, St Mark's Square, Venice, Credit: Giraudon. Page 27, Claude Monet, *Palazzo de Mula, Venice*, Credit: Exley/Rosenthal. Page 28, Photograph of Monet in his garden, Credit: Corbis. Page 29, Claude Monet, *Waterlilies*, Credit: Giraudon.

Cover photograph reproduced with permission of Bridgeman Art Library

Our thanks to Paul Flux for his comments in the preparation of this book.

Every effort has been made to contact copyright holders of any material reproduced in this book. Any omissions will be rectified in subsequent printings if notice is given to the Publisher.

Some words in this book are in bold, **like this.** You can find out what they mean by looking in the glossary.

Contents

Who Was Claude Monet?

Claude Monet was a French artist. He was one of the **Impressionists**. These painters tried to show the change of light through the day in their paintings.

4

Claude painted the same **scene** many times to show the change of light. This painting shows clouds **reflected** in the lily pond in his garden.

Early Years

Claude Oscar Monet was born in Paris, France on November 14, 1840. His family soon moved to the **port** of Le Havre. Claude liked being near the sea.

Claude liked the way light showed on water.
This drawing shows the coast near Le Havre.
Claude drew it when he was 24 years old.

School Days

Claude did not like school. He made clever **caricatures** of his classmates. A local painter named Eugène Boudin saw these drawings. He wanted Claude to become a painter.

Claude could pick out the important things to draw. He was 16 years old when he made this funny drawing of a young man dressed in stylish clothes.

Making Friends

In 1861, Claude joined the army but became ill after a year. His family gave him some money to become a painter. Claude moved to Paris when he was 22 years old.

10

Claude became close friends with other young artists in Paris. They often painted together. Claude painted this **scene** on a trip to the countryside near Paris.

Living in London

In 1870, Claude married Camille Doncieux. Since France was at war with Germany, Paris was dangerous. Claude and his wife moved to London, England. This picture shows how London looked then.

Claude and his wife lived for a while in London.
Claude saw many paintings by English artists.
He painted the Thames River many times while
he was in London.

Discovering Light

In 1871, Claude moved back to France. He built a floating **studio** to study how light affects water. This painting by an artist named Manet shows Claude in his floating studio.

Claude liked to paint outside in every season. This painting shows a street in winter. He painted it in 1875.

The Impressionists

Claude and his friends painted quickly. Most **galleries** thought their paintings looked messy. In 1874, Claude and his friends **exhibited** their paintings in a building on this street.

This group of painters became known as the **Impressionists**. The name came from the title of this painting by Claude called *Impression, Sunrise*. He painted this harbor just after **dawn**.

Two Families

Claude and his family moved in with their friend Alice Hoschede and her children. Claude now had to look after two families and eight children.

Claude began to paint what he saw near his
new home. He used quick **strokes** of the brush
to show light and shape.

Giverny

In 1879, Claude's wife, Camille, died. Later, Claude married his friend Alice. Their families moved to Giverny, near Paris. Claude loved his new garden. He also painted in the countryside near his home.

20

Claude worked quickly. He painted the same **scenes** over and over. This painting tells us about the houses, fields, and weather one afternoon.

Painting Trips

During the 1880s, Claude spent many months away from home each year. He traveled around France and painted many **landscapes**. He worked in all kinds of weather.

This painting shows the seashore in southern France. Claude used quick **brushwork**. You can almost feel the wind blowing through the trees and across the sea.

Series Paintings

Claude painted the same **scenes** at different times. Together these pictures are known as his **series paintings**. He painted this **cathedral** many times. It is in Rouen, France.

Claude loved to paint the front of Rouen Cathedral. It is almost hidden by mist in this painting. Other paintings by Monet show the Cathedral in bright sunlight.

Travels

Claude made his last painting trips when he was over 60 years old. He traveled to Spain, Holland, England, and Italy. This photograph shows Claude and Alice in Venice, Italy.

Claude loved the buildings in Venice. They rose straight out of the water. This painting shows a beautiful palace **reflected** in the water.

Waterlilies

Claude spent his last years at home in Giverny. He still thought about light and shape. He died on December 5, 1926. He was 86 years old. The other **Impressionists** had died long before that.

Many of Claude's last works were huge paintings of waterlilies. In this painting it is hard to tell where the lilies end and their **reflections** begin.

Timeline

1840	Claude Monet born, November 14
1857	Claude meets the painter Eugène Boudin
1862	Claude moves to Paris to become a painter
1865	American Civil War ends
1865–6	Claude has paintings shown to the public in Paris
1870	Claude marries Camille Doncieux and lives in London
1870–71	War between France and Germany
1871	Claude moves to a new house in Argenteuil, France
1874	Claude helps set up the first **exhibit** by the **Impressionists**
1876	The telephone is invented
1879	Camille dies
1883	Claude moves to Giverny
1893	Claude begins building a pond in the garden at Giverny
1909	First public **exhibit** of Claude's waterlily paintings
1914–18	**World War I**
1926	Claude Monet dies, December 5

Glossary

brushwork   marks left by an artist's paint brush

caricature   funny drawing of someone

cathedral   large church

dawn   when it starts to get light in the morning

exhibit   to show artwork in public

gallery   place where works of art are shown and sold

Impressionists   group of artists who painted outside to make colorful pictures

landscape   painting of the countryside

port   city on the edge of the ocean

reflect   give a second picture of something, as with a mirror

scene   place where something happens

series painting   painting of the same thing but painted at different times

stroke   mark made by one movement of the brush

studio   place where an artist works

World War I   war in Europe that lasted from 1914 –1918

Index

More Books to Read

Halliwell , Sarah. *Impressionism & Postimpressionism: Artists, Writers & Composers.* Austin, Tex. : Raintree Steck-Vaughn, 1998.

Koju , Stephan, and Katja Miksovsky. *Claude Monet: The Magician of Colour.* New York: te Neues Publishing, 1997.

An older reader can help you with these books.

More Artwork to See

Boulevard des Capucines, 1873–74. Nelson-Atkins Museum of Art, Kansas City, MO.

The Japanese Footbridge, 1899. National Gallery of Art, Washington, D.C.

The Rose Covered Pergola, Giverny, 1913. Phoenix Art Museum, Phoenix, Ariz.